C000227247

NATURE IN MINIATURE

NATURE IN MINIATURE

Andreas Feininger

THAMES AND HUDSON

First published in Great Britain in 1989 by
Thames and Hudson Ltd, London

First published in the United States of America in 1989 by
Rizzoli International Publications, Inc.

Designed by Solveig Williams
Set in type by Roberts/Churcher
Printed and bound in Singapore

Contents

Introduction   6

Color   14

In the Woods   38

Design   64

On the Beach   92

Symbolism and Imagination   118

Epilogue   140

Introduction

Staghorn sumach leaves in fall appear to glow with the last of summer's heat.

I am a photographer possessed by the magic and mystery of nature. Although a considerable amount of my work has been done in cities, my main interest lies in the various aspects of nature that form the subject matter of this book. This is where I feel at home, this is what I live for—that indescribable, all-pervasive feeling of being a living, active, thinking part of something immense.

For twenty years I worked as a staff photographer for *LIFE* magazine; then followed a period when I wrote text books on photographic subjects and made documentary photographs for picture books. Now I have finally reached a point where I can let my imagination run free—I can choose my own topics, create my own images, give tangible expression to my own feelings, and use the picture language of photography as a means of "talking" to people with whom I want to share experiences important to me, which, after all, is the reason why I photograph.

This collection—of mostly recent but also older work—is such an exercise, a product of this freedom. Every photograph in it is a personal statement; each image was created with a specific idea in mind—which I will elaborate on in the following chapters. But they also, seen as a whole, represent a larger personal vision, my belief that nature needs to be studied intimately, that by focusing in on the mystery of its minute designs, man can better understand his own position in the universal cycle.

When we speak of nature, the images that automatically come to mind are those of scenery: meadows and mountains, forests and lakes, the sea. . . . In other words, we tend to think in sweeping terms—seeing the large, more or less amorphous forms of hills and trees. The reason for this, I believe, is that the average person's contact with nature is usually not as close as his or her involvement with the more familiar works of man. As a result of this approach, many people miss the particular kind of beauty that becomes apparent only if nature's creations are experienced from close up. For it is a fact that the closer we approach, the more detail we see, and it is usually in their details that objects of nature are at their most fascinating, no matter whether the observer is interested primarily in structure, the relationship between function and form, or in beauty.

Whenever possible, I like my photographs to show *more* than the viewer would and often could have seen in reality. I do this with the aid of magnifying telephoto and close-up lenses that can produce clear images of objects too far away or too small to be perceived by the unaided eye; controlled lighting to reveal significant, but under ordinary conditions unobtrusive, texture and detail; an unusual perspective or angle of view; a decisive cropping to exclude extraneous pictorial matter; exaggerated contrast; or other graphic aids suitable for emphasizing characteristic designs. In this way, the image becomes an interpretive rather than documentary photograph, concerned more with conveying an intangible feeling or mood than with reproducing a fact. In my experience, a documentary-realistic rendition that shows the subject exactly as it appeared to the eye is often boring, no matter how interesting the subject itself, because it only repeats what the viewer has already seen before. But a picture that gives him or her something new to behold, although it may at first appear unfamiliar and be rejected as "unnatural," will slowly assert itself and eventually be accepted and even appreciated because it is stimulating.

The first prerequisite for making effective photographs is interest in the subject. Interest is the spark that ignites the photographer's creative potential. It is the reason why we photograph. It marks the moment of conception of the future picture. Visions arise, images take shape in the photographer's mind, the idea for a picture is born. Interest engenders enthusiasm without which the entire process of picture making sinks to the level of technical routine. And while nobody can create great photographs without mastering photo-technique, to judge a photograph on the basis of technical excellence

Section of the
discarded skin of a
snake.

10

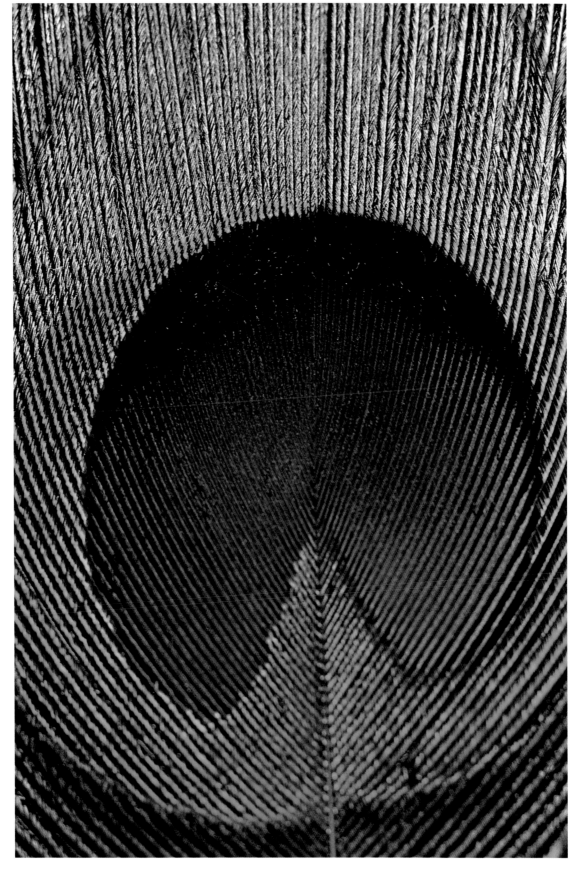

alone is as naive as judging a novel by the correctness of its syntax. A technically perfect photograph can be the world's most boring picture, whereas a good photographic concept—an interesting subject interestingly seen—can be conveyed even through a technically poor rendition. The subject's interest will still be there and the picture will speak to the viewer, however haltingly.

Nature as a subject for photography may be classified in two ways. The first comprises those objects that possess photogenic qualities—simplicity, clarity, characteristic forms, interesting outlines, bold and graphic designs, high or low contrasts, spontaneity or movement. These are infinitely photographable. The second group of subjects in nature I call "the unphotographables." These are basically interesting subjects that, because of circumstances not directly related to them—unsuitable backgrounds, bad lighting, persistent wind in shots requiring long exposure times—would result in disappointing pictures.

Here is a recent example: I was walking with a friend on a foggy morning in fall. All around us spider webs, made visible by droplets of dew, covered the ground like lacy handkerchiefs. "This is magic. . . ." my companion said to me, "why don't you photograph it?" I explained that this was one of the "unphotographable" subjects, but couldn't convince her. She took out her own camera and made a shot. Later, when contemplating the result, she admitted, "You were right, this looks only like a litter-covered field. . . ." In this case, successful rendition of this lovely phenomenon was impossible because a close-up would have failed to convey the feeling of "masses of little lace handkerchiefs," while an overall shot would have rendered the individual webs too small to be identifiable.

Photographing such a sensitive phenomenon in order to realistically document its beauty would, in fact require a great deal of technical manipulation. This book, however, is not concerned with the traditional documentation of the wonders of nature. My aim has been instead to convey to the viewer intangibles, like the thoughts and feelings that motivated me to make these pictures: the joy of finding beauty, fascinating forms, delicate details, or thought-provoking aspects in common objects of nature. In the course of this journey of visual exploration I made many stimulating discoveries: I saw monumentality in the shapes of broken shells, small animal skulls became idols consecrated to demons or spirits of the forest, butterfly wing designs and flower petals overwhelmed me with the richness of their glorious color, pieces of driftwood evoked erotic images, fragments of eroded clam shells reminded me of ancient friezes, strange markings on caterpillars revealed themselves as highly effective means of protection from potential predators, the colors of turning leaves in fall rivaled in range and inventiveness the best in modern abstract art, slices of agate suggested unearthly landscapes, seas, and skies.

Although photography continues to be my language—the language of vision—I do no longer photograph. Now that I am past eighty, I have given away my cameras and other photographic equipment. At first, it felt strange to walk the woods without a camera handy, in case. . . . But gradually this feeling of being "naked" has given way to one of quiet contemplation and inner peace. Now I can more fully enjoy the things that move me because I don't have to see them any longer from the photographer's point of view: how is the light? is the background suitable? and what about the angle of view. . . ? Because, in the past, only too often one or more of these factors had been so unsatisfactory, so frustrating that I held back from photographing even the most photogenic subject rather than compromise and waste my time, energy, and film on a shot that I would only destroy later. Now I can enjoy even these "unphotographables," and my life has become the richer for it.

Color

Few flowers reach, and none surpass in burning intensity, the color of transluminated petals of red tulips.

Man's use of color on a large scale tends to be either drab or garish—too little or too much. The overall impression created by big city streets contrasts jarringly with the screaming color outburst of advertising and the "neon jungle"—confronting one with either battleship-gray monotony or psychedelic hysteria.

In contrast, the effect of large-scale color displays in nature is completely different. Nature's colors, too, are often monotonous, as for example a uniformly blue sky or a wide open expanse of green or tan. But unlike the color monotony of city streets, which I find depressing, color monotony in nature has a gently pleasing effect on me, soothing and positive. If manifested in the form of miles and miles of forest-covered hills, green symbolizes to me serenity and eternity and makes me feel at peace with myself. However, painted on indoor walls, it reminds me of school days and becomes a symbol for institutional bureaucracy. And the same shade of pink that delights me in a wild flower, or the delicate chartreuse of fresh young leaves, looks cheap to me when found in artifacts.

Except for flaming sunset skies and volcanic eruptions, color at its concentrated best is found in the smaller objects of nature. Nothing comes even close in intensity to the deep velvety purple of petunias, the fire-engine red of tulips, the radiant yellow of dandelions, or the azure blue of gentians. Combinations of different colors, surpassing in beauty the efforts of most modern painters, can be found in the designs of butterfly wings. Gem stones and certain minerals are further sources of brilliant color, as are the feathers of many birds. Even such lowly objects as decaying leaves can present exciting patterns in bright as well as subtle shades of brown, green, yellow, orange, red, and even gray and black. Indeed, some decaying leaves that I have picked up from the ground are among the most beautiful objects of my collection, their color schemes reminiscent of abstract paintings. When enlarged, such small objects have the power to surprise and delight.

In autumn, the sensitive eye finds beauty and harmony even among fallen leaves not blazing in yellow and red.

Five staghorn sumach
leaflets in fall.

A fall collection of sugar maple leaves.

A single leaf of red
maple in fall can
transform a carpet of
ordinary white ash
leaves into an
aesthetic experience.

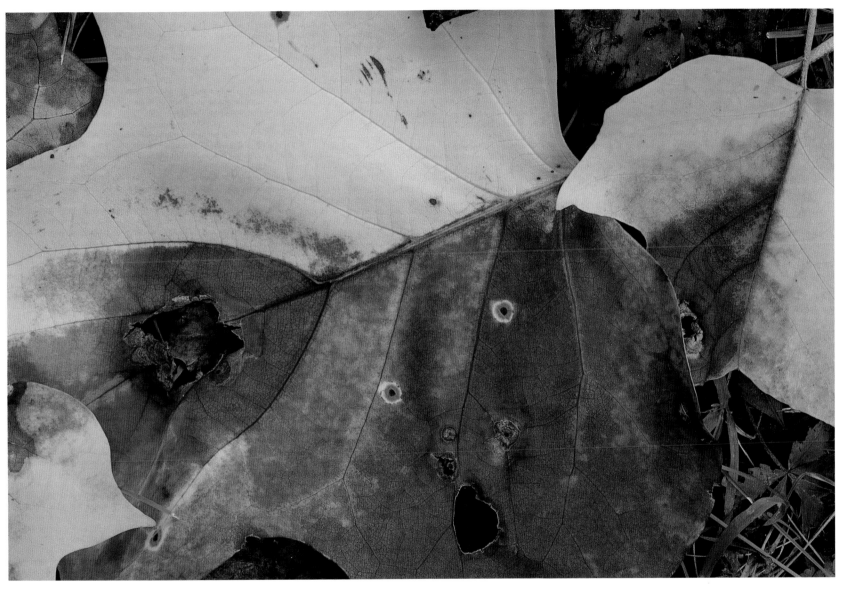

A fallen tulip tree leaf, bold in concept and color, reminds me of certain works of modern abstract art.

Raindrops glitter like diamonds on a wilted leaflet of
Virginia creeper in fall.

These are autumn's somber hues displayed in leaves of sugar maple, Virginia creeper, black oak, and hickory in various states of decay.

Red maple leaves in
September, turning
purple, still cling to
the tree.

Two weeks later, on the ground, these same leaves form a carpet fit for a king.

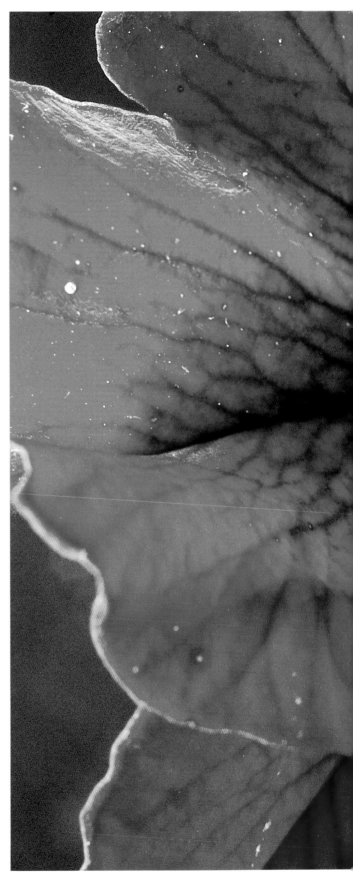

The velvety texture and deeply saturated colors of
petunias put man-made fabrics to shame.

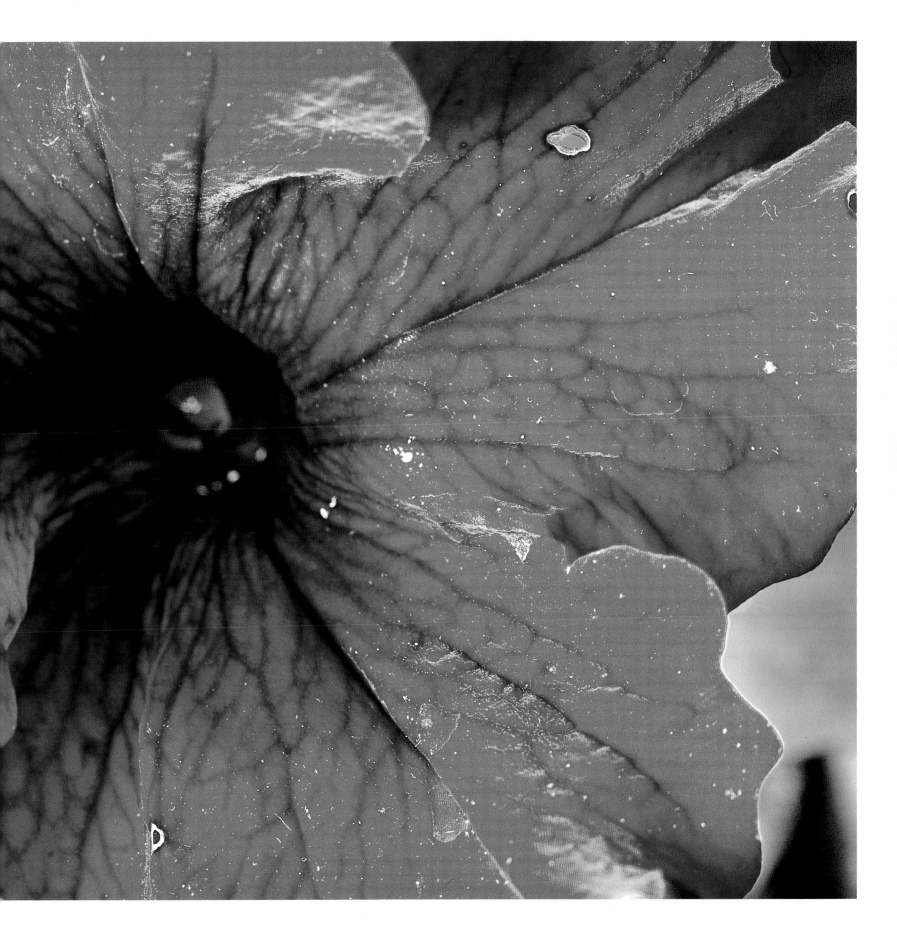

Close-ups of tropical butterfly wings. Each of their microscopically small scales has only a single color. Effects of "shading" are created by aggregates of scales in different colors, producing a Pointillistic design analogous to the image on a television screen.

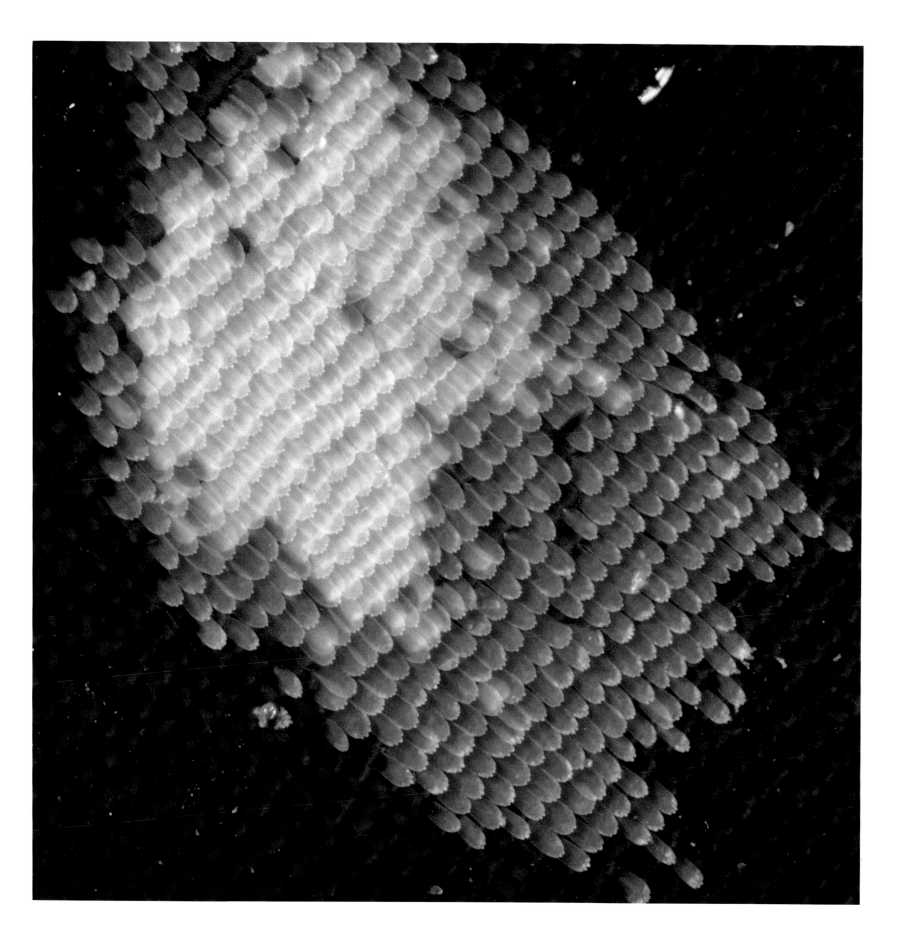

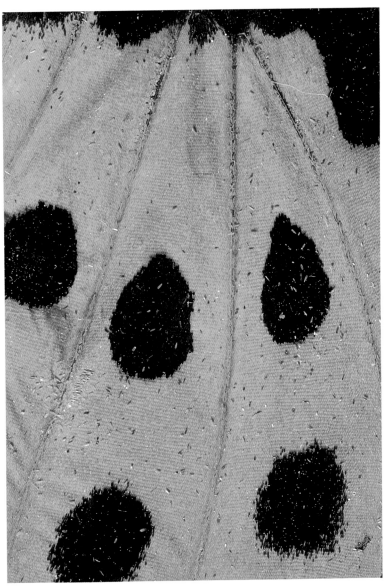

The differently colored scales of butterfly wings are never randomly distributed but form specific designs, each pattern characteristic of a single species. The aesthetic effect can be breathtakingly beautiful.

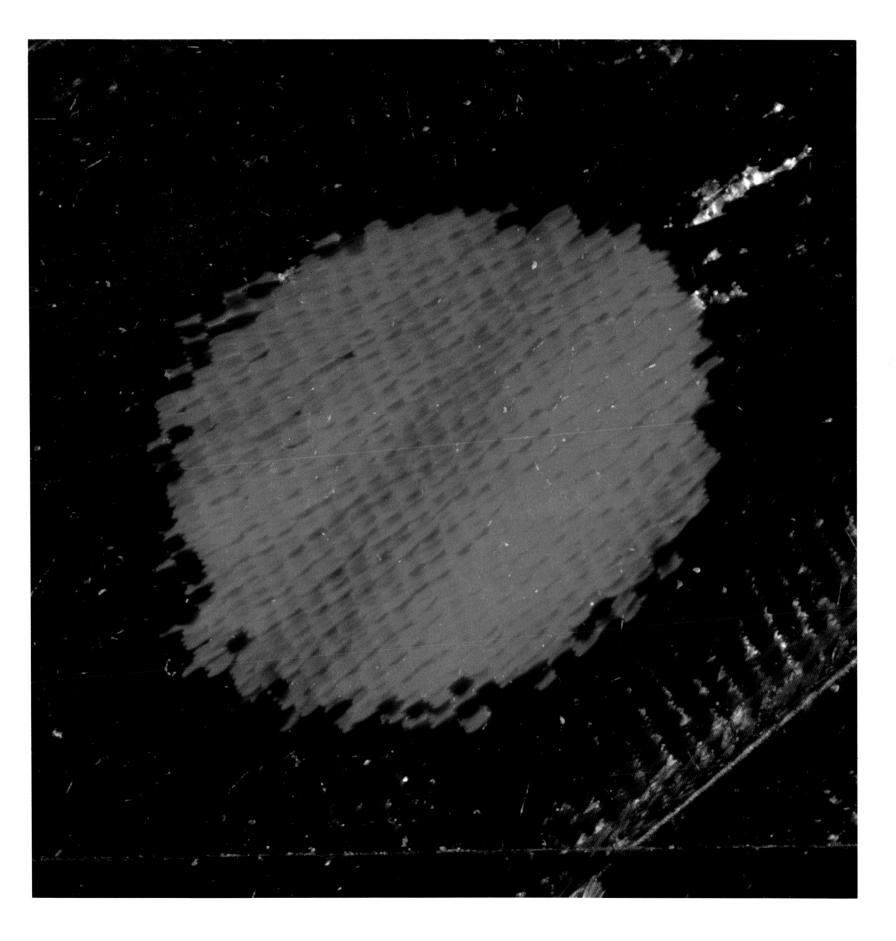

Close-up of the front wing of an unspecified butterfly.
Names are mainly for scientists; important here is the
artistic-aesthetic effect regardless of the insect's name.

Butterfly wing scales strongly magnified. Like shingles covering a roof, these delicate objects, each in a single solid color, form the patterns that so often delight our eyes.

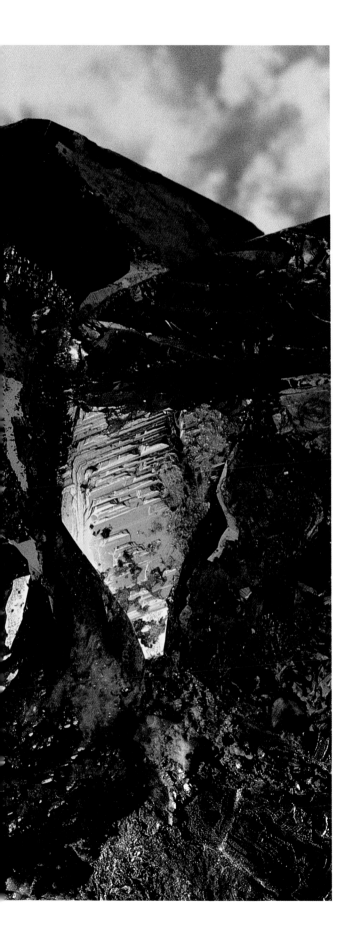

Crystals of pyrite or fool's gold, a common mineral. Actually only a few inches high, their inherent monumentality is brought out here through appropriate camera angle and lighting.

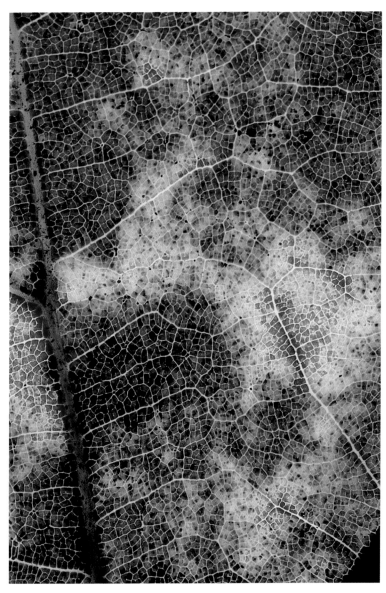

Sugar maple leaves in fall. The effect is not unlike that of aerial photographs of farmland, of fields transversed by main and secondary roads.

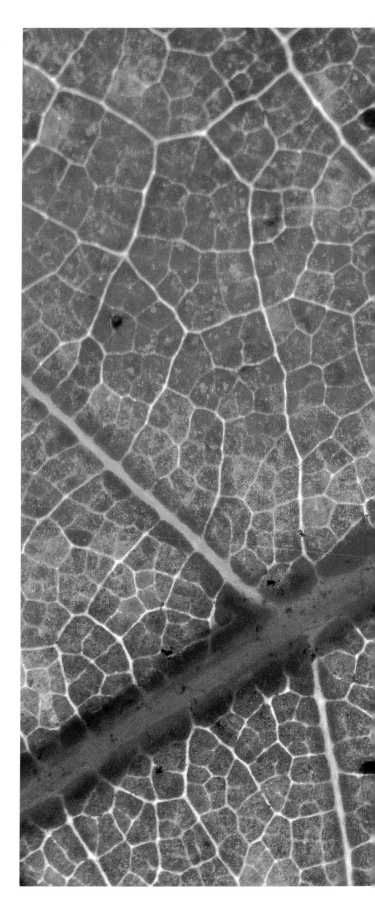

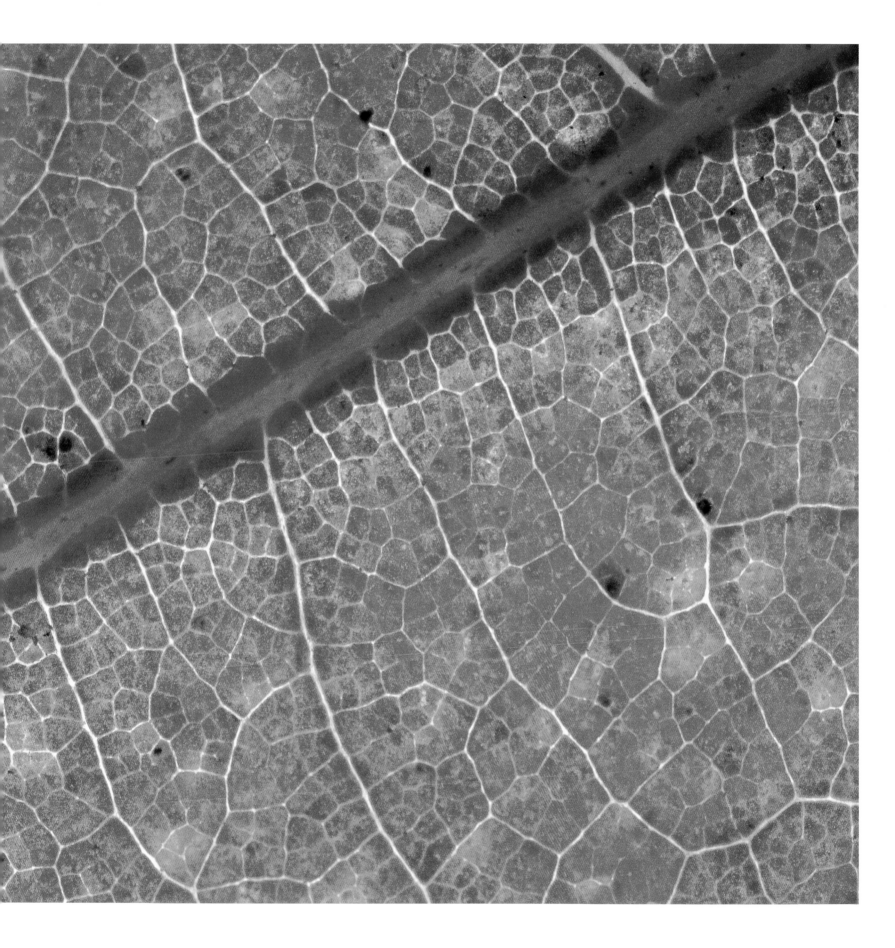

In the Woods

Sunlight on sassafras leaves transforms a normally ordinary event into an artistically exciting experience symbolic of spring.

38

A forest is a self-contained ecosystem in which everything affects, and is in turn affected by, everything else. The tiniest creatures play roles in determining the character of a woods, along with the composition and slope of the soil, the underground water supply, the orientation to the sun, the altitude, and atmospheric factors such as temperature, rainfall, and humidity. Observing the interaction of these various elements has been to me a never-ending source of inspiration.

Dead organisms return to the soil where decaying processes dissociate their substances into basic compounds that furnish building blocks for new life. This chain reaction is initiated by fungi and bacteria, which liberate essential chemicals for use by plants. These plants are then eaten by herbivorous animals who in turn provide food for the flesh-eaters, and ultimately man. This is recycling on a cosmic scale—a form of immortality.

But what fascinates me about the never-ending cycle of the forest is that it reveals nature as infinitely more adaptable than man. Nature will change itself, over years, perhaps centuries, in order to better work within the system. Whereas man would rather change the system than adapt himself to it— rather cut down the woods than learn to live with them. Nature's experiments with camouflage are perfect examples. One day, walking along a trail in the woods I noticed a dark brown butterfly fluttering ahead of me. I tried to get a closer look, but suddenly the insect disappeared. Where did it go? How could this have happened while I was watching it? Then I found it again, sitting right in front of me among some dead leaves. It had folded its gorgeous wings above its back, straight up, so that seen from either front or rear they were all but invisible, paper-thin, while from the side, their pattern blended so well with the surrounding flickering light and shadow that it was a surprise that I noticed the insect at all. A marvelous example of camouflage.

The wing patterns of certain tropical butterflies show an equally clever response to their environment. They imitate foliage so perfectly that they even

Like the entrance to a mysterious cave, this opening among the branches of a spruce invites the curious mind to penetrate the secrets of the woods.

41

show the center rib of a leaf. In addition, the form of the wing is such that this rib actually ends in the most convincing imitation of a leaf stalk which, when the insect is resting, touches the twig on which it sits. Even at a distance of only a few inches, these butterflies are virtually unrecognizable as insects, having turned into "leaves."

The inchworm caterpillar, too, can transform itself. In appearance, it looks exactly like a twig, complete with all a twig's irregularities and a head formed like a little bud. When alarmed, it suddenly straightens, becomes rigid, lets go with its front legs, and sticks out at an angle relative to its perch, thus becoming a "twig."

The best deception artists, however, are the moths that come in many different species, sizes, and designs. They all have one thing in common: their wing pattern and coloration either imitate tree bark so convincingly that the resting insect becomes invisible, or they are an obtrusive flash of white, which makes them stand out and look exactly like bird droppings on a green leaf.

Such miraculous adaptations are the results of evolution: insects that were conspicuous fell easy prey to predators, while those with subtler coloring were more difficult to find, and so survived in larger numbers to propagate their kind. While this camouflage concept can be explained scientifically, the millions of years of accidental mutations, of trial and error, leave it still bordering on the miraculous to me.

Every walk I take in the forest provides me with a new experience. No two days are ever exactly alike. On a dew-fresh morning, spiderwebs are transformed into strings of pearls, glitter like diamonds, each droplet refracting the sunlight into needle-thin beams of the most intense spectral colors—ruby red, sapphire blue, emerald green—instantly changing from one hue to another as I move my eyes. Spider webs present a considerable photographic challenge. Unfortunately, most webs are torn almost as soon as they are finished—by struggling insects, bumble bees that fly right through

Orb spider web, one of nature's most fascinating creations.

them, or wind-ruffled twigs and leaves—and so it is hard to do justice to their exquisite design. Compounding this, spider silk is so fine that it is invisible unless seen in backlight or when droplets of dew clinging to the strands catch the sunlight. The only lighting that illuminates the delicate structure of an orb web in its entirety is backlight; light from any other direction would reflect from only certain strands, leaving the rest invisible. Furthermore, the background must be dark and uniform in tone; otherwise light spots would ruin the impression of the web, which would appear tattered or incomplete. And finally, the air must be perfectly still since even the slightest draft would cause the delicate strands to flutter. Since a close-up is necessary to capture the fine detail, the lens has to be stopped down considerably to achieve adequate sharpness in depth which in turn requires relatively long exposures during which the slightest move of a strand would cause a blur in the rendition. But more than exquisite creations, spider webs are sophisticated manifestations of the mysterious power of instinct—no parents taught their offsprings these web-spinning skills, they are inherited. Instinct is an inborn pattern of activity or tendency to action. What puzzles me is that something intangible—a quality that is not material—can be inherited and transmitted from generation to generation. And, interestingly, we find this magic force to action in all the lower animals, but it is much rarer in higher forms of life.

Certain solitary wasps excavate small underground cells in which they deposit their eggs. These hideouts are then stocked with food for the emerging grub in the form of caterpillars or spiders anesthetized by a poisonous sting administered in exactly the right spot. This technique, too, is inherited—a technique requiring astonishingly detailed anatomical knowledge of the insect's prey: the slightest miscalculation, and the prey either remains so lively that it might hurt or kill the grub; or it dies, decomposes, and the grub perishes of starvation. While science maintains that the cause of this efficiency is the fact that everything is done instinctively, that insects have no choice and are like programmed automatons, incapable of acting any other way, it is also true that some species communicate with one another, exchange information about food supplies, unite to fight off invaders, and that at least ants conduct wars with other tribes.

And if animals can possess instincts, why not plants? After all, they, too, are alive. For example, what kind of force makes a plant, from lowly weed to stately tree, grow against the force of gravity and thereby contradict the force of entropy? And why is it that plants keep on increasing in volume and height until they die, while animals, having reached maturity, stop growing? It probably has to do with the fact that a tree, at least theoretically, can increase in bulk indefinitely because it is stationary and supported by solid ground. On the other hand, an animal grown beyond a certain size, would collapse under its own weight the moment it rises and starts to move.

To me, these interactions are further proof that all of nature's components are in finely tuned equilibrium—that is, provided there is no interference from man. Unless man learns from the harmonious cycle of the forest, and begins to act accordingly, he cannot survive.

Spider webs. Spider silk is too fine to be visible to the unaided human eye unless accentuated by backlight or droplets of dew. Each species produces its own characteristic design, a talent that is inherited. No parents taught young spiders how to spin their webs.

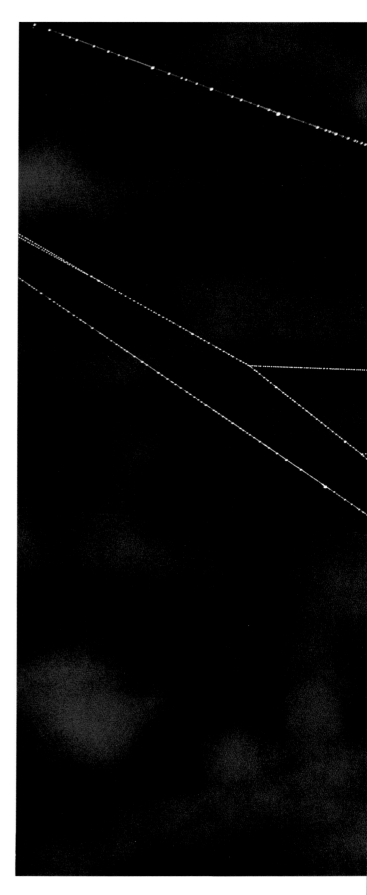

Caterpillar of an unspecified moth. Although abhorrent
to most people, many caterpillars, when seen close up,
are really very beautiful and often fantastic in regard to
design.

The snowy white of this moth is actually a form of camouflage: when resting on a leaf, it resembles a piece of bird dropping, fooling predators who pass it up.

Droplets of rain or dew can transform common objects
of nature into sparkling jewelry.

Left: Lichen, a strange plant organism consisting of an alga and a fungus living together in true symbiosis; neither one could exist alone without the other's help. *Right:* A nocturnal moth so perfectly camouflaged that it is virtually invisible when resting on bark where it spends the day.

Another example of camouflage: the markings on a
caterpillar of a sphinx moth (*right*) resemble fungi
growing on dead wood (*left*) to such a degree that
predators are easily fooled and leave the caterpillar alone.

Fungi—a shelf fungus (*above*) and a mushroom partly eaten by snails (*right*)—because they contain no chlorophyll, are unable to produce their own food and must lead parasitic lives. However, they are indispensable to the welfare of their environment because, together with bacteria, they decompose dead plant material, free carbon dioxide, recycle basic chemicals, and keep the quality of humus high.

56

Puffballs, a spherical form of fungus which emits
smokelike clouds of microscopically small spores when
ripe.

Entrance to the nest of a solitary wasp. Details of this fascinating insect's life have been discussed on page 44.

Tulip tree leaf
unfolding in spring
from its winter bud.

A piece of pine bark into which beetle grubs have carved their tunnels, leaving a decorative design.

Above: Blue jay feathers on mossy ground. *Right:* Leaf
arrangement of staghorn sumach. Leaves never grow
randomly but are always organized in such a way that
they cast as little shadow as possible on their neighbors.
The resulting pattern is called a leaf mosaic.

Design

Dendrite—traces left by mineralized solutions which
penetrated a crack in the rock where they crystallized.
The resulting lines never cross or even touch each other;
the reason for this strange behavior is unknown.

It is as if a great designer has been at work wherever I look or probe in nature, a supernatural intelligence that pervades the universe. The word "design" can refer either to the physical-structural or the visual-artistic aspects of an object. Because I am a photographer as well as a former architect and engineer, both these aspects in nature appeal to me. In previous books I have dealt extensively with the structural design of nature's creations; here, I would like to emphasize some of their visual-artistic qualities.

While it is easy to talk unequivocally about the structural characteristics of an object, to make a valid judgment about its artistic merits is quite another matter. Such an evaluation can never be more than a subjective opinion, because what moves one person may leave another one cold. In many people's minds, the works of nature, in contrast to those of man, seem somehow amorphous, a difference perhaps analagous to that between a building and a tree: on one side, straight lines, right angles, and geometrically clean-cut forms; on the other, soft outlines and ever-changing shapes. This, however, is only partly true.

Two concepts associated with the works of man, but unexpected in nature, are those of symmetry and geometrically precise forms. The reason is probably that they manifest themselves abundantly in our civilized environment on a scale large enough to be easily noticed. While in nature, the qualifying objects are often unobtrusive or small.

Symmetry occurs in nature in either lateral, radial, or spherical form. The bodies of mammals, birds, and butterflies are laterally symmetrical; flowers like asters, daisies, or clematis, and animals like starfish or jellyfish are constructed on the principle of radial symmetry; and the seed crowns of daisies and allium are spherically symmetrical.

Each of these forms is executed with a consistency and perfection that makes me wonder about the force that rules their growth. Do the left wings of a butterfly "know" how the wings on the right side look so that they can match them precisely, down to the last detail? What mechanism divides some flowers into four, five, six, eight, or more identical sectors, as accurately as if these patterns were laid out with a divider?

The geometrically precise forms that commonly occur in nature are spirals, ovoids, and ellipsoids. Beautifully executed spirals are produced by many gastropods (sea shells and snails) and, of course, that paragon, the chambered nautilus. In plants, too, spiral growth is quite common: vines, the tentacles of passion flowers and other clinging plants, and the arrangement of leaves on a stem or axis, all rotate in single or double spirals.

Ovoids, or egg forms, are equally fascinating. Every time I see a bird's egg I am amazed by the incredibly precise curves of these often only paper-thin shells. I wonder what kind of mechanism produces such perfect forms within the body of a bird, forms whose beauty is not only visual but also sensual.

Ellipsoids are three-dimensional solids whose plane sections are ellipses. I have a collection of these beautiful shapes in the form of granite pebbles, ground and polished by the surf. Their contours are so symmetrical that it is hard to believe they have not been finished by some expert craftsman. Holding these, preferably sun-warmed, stones between my hands, closing my eyes, and exploring their curves by touch alone, is a unique sensual experience.

Butterfly wings are rightly considered to be among the most exquisite of nature's designs. The variety of their patterns is unlimited, their colors are among the most beautiful on earth. Although these colors seem to grade smoothly from one hue to another, they are in fact built up of minute scales, each with only a single, solid color. Creation of the overall effect of one color flowing smoothly into another is like that of a Pointillist painting or the image on a television screen, both of which also consist of minute dots of color.

Leaves are an endless source of fascinating, natural designs. Two aspects

Tulip tree leaves in fall.

Leaves from a dying weed form aesthetically interesting designs.

Blue jay feather.

of their characteristics in particular should attract anyone searching for beauty and order in nature: outline and color. While some of nature's more spectacular designs are rare, leaves can be found everywhere, and some of the most common species of non-woody plants as well as trees have some of the most artistically satisfying designs. Their arrangement on a branch, while apparently random, is always in accordance with the need of the respective plant for light—its life-giving, indispensable energy source. Consequently, leaves grow only in specific patterns called leaf-mosaics which assure that these ingenious food factories shade one another as little as possible, thereby providing each leaf with a maximum of light. Studying these leaf-mosaics and observing how different plants have solved this problem by adjusting their various growth patterns, leaf sizes, and forms has given me many hours of thought-provoking pleasure and a sense of universal unity based upon the realization that everything in nature is dependent on everything else.

The design of pine cones also intrigues me. I admire the way the seed-bearing scales are organized in the form of two sets of interpenetrating spirals, one curving in the opposite direction from the other, forming a geometrically and aesthetically pleasing design. But what is particularly fascinating to me—I am now speaking as an architect and engineer—is the fact that the number of spirals in each set almost always coincides with adjoining numbers of the Fibonacci series, the mathematical progression in which each number is the sum of the two preceding numbers: 1,1,2,3,5,8,13,21, and so on. Thus mathematics and geometry rule the growth of plants through the arrangement of their molecules.

The design of a feather is both a structural and an artistic feat of genius. It is not only "featherlight" but also inordinately strong. Its thermal insulating power against heat and cold rivals that of the best synthetic materials. A feather consists of a "backbone"—the hollow shaft or quill—which carries two sets of slender, interlocking barbs. Each barb is equipped with even finer side branches—the barbules—which in turn carry still smaller branches—the barbicles. Finally, the barbicles are covered with countless, microscopically small hooks which, like the teeth of a zipper, hold everything together. Altogether, a feather may consist of several million parts, each executed to standards of unimaginable perfection. The complete unit forms an essentially flat, though slightly twisted and curved, highly elastic air foil. As far as efficiency of design and precision of execution are concerned, no man-made object comes even close.

When it comes to depicting delicate objects like feathers, however, photography reveals itself once more as the crude medium of rendition that it really is. No picture can do a feather justice and convey that indescribable feeling of elasticity combined with strength, express the exquisite three-dimensional beauty of the smartly curving shaft, or impart its sensuous softness when touched. The only way I can really experience a feather is to handle it, and then I begin to wonder. . . . A featherless bird cannot fly, nor could any developing species of animal wait for evolution to transform its fur into feathers. And yet bats can fly without the aid of feathers. Why then did evolving birds not stick to proven membrane-covered wings? What caused nature to invent the feather—a process that must have taken hundreds of thousands of years before it was perfected to the point where it enabled birds to fly?

Nature has this effect on me; it stimulates a continuous flow of contemplation and questioning. After several decades of close study, nature still has the power to stir my imagination and heighten my sense of wonder.

Blue jay feathers.

Feathers from a
flicker, a member of
the woodpecker
family.

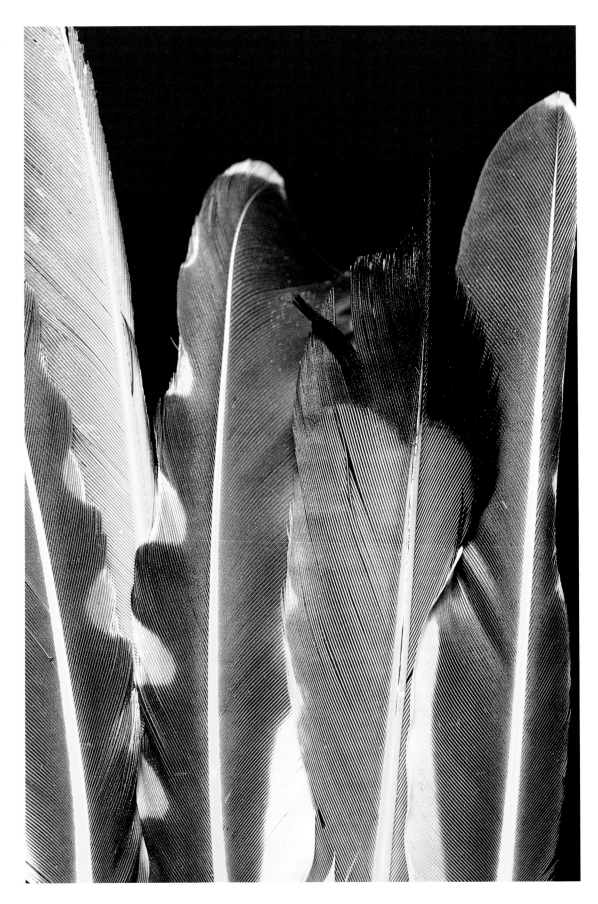

Spider
chrysanthemum.

Allium, a spherical-
symmetrical flower. A
window cut into the
seed crown exposes
the exquisitely
engineered internal
structure.

Land snails from Puerto Rico; a collection of empty shells.

Chambered nautilus, sectioned shell and outside view.
To imagine that an allegedly "slimy" mollusk created
this magnificent, hard and crystalline, geometrically
nearly perfect construct is almost beyond belief.

Pine cone. The number of opposing spirals is 8 and 13, a pair from the Fibonacci series, a mathematical progression explained on page 71.

Wilted hickory leaves form a powerful, aesthetically attractive, sculptural design.

Two dendrites. The variety of these elegant patterns is infinite. In reality, each of the two specimens shown here is approximately two inches wide.

Butterfly wing details. Marvelous, how the close-up lens
reveals detail invisible to the unaided human eye. In
nature, the closer we look, the more discoveries we
make, finding marvels in structures which, in regard to
precision of execution, make the finest human artifacts
look crude.

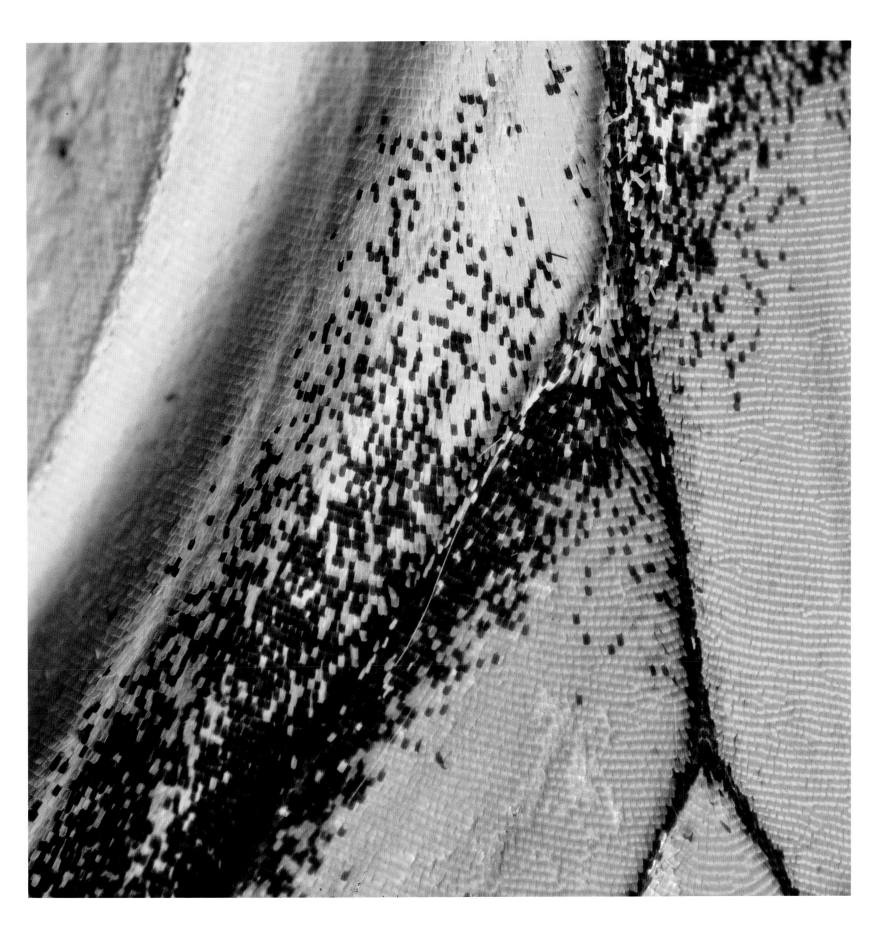

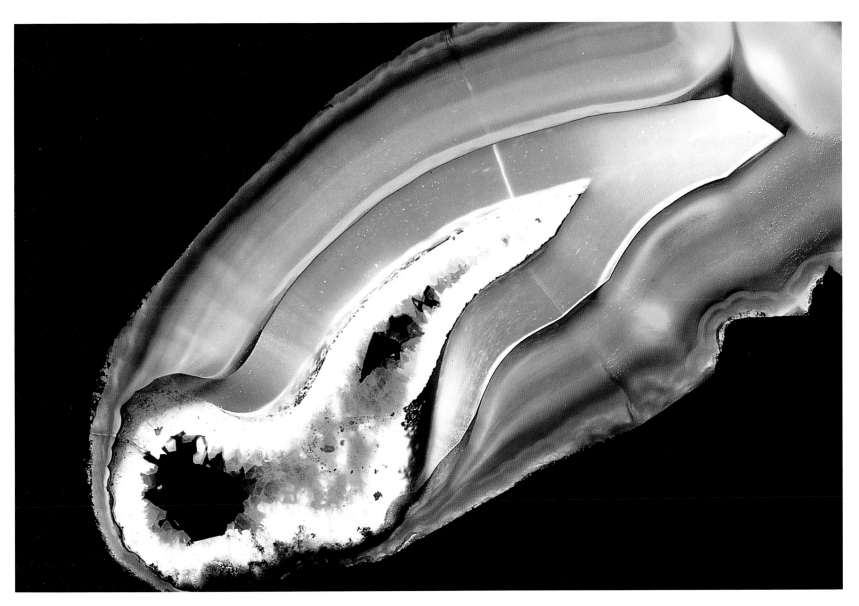

Thin slices of agate seen in transmitted light

Above: Marvel at the precision of execution of these milfoil leaves, a common "weed."

Right: A Virginia creeper vine delights us with the perfectly symmetrical, evenly spaced arrangement of its leaves.

On the Beach

A close look at the beach near Bradenton on the Gulf Coast of Florida.

If I could choose a place to spend the rest of my life, it would have to be near a wide, sandy beach. Perhaps it is the memory of carefree childhood days which makes this kind of landscape so attractive to me. Perhaps it is an atavistic force that draws me back to the place where all life began—the sea.

I try to analyze the power of the sea and beach over me. It is a many faceted force: the open spaces, wide horizons, and clean, salty air. I love to walk fast and roam over wide and unobstructed ground not yet defiled by man. I love the hiss of the surf and the thunder of breaking waves. I love the loneliness and grandeur of an empty beach. I love the calls of terns and gulls—perhaps the most independent, resourceful, and toughest of all birds. And especially, I love the excitement of finding unexpected treasures among the winding windrows of wrack cast up by the sea.

My treasures have no monetary value and probably would be dismissed by most people who take to the beach as "trash." But to me, even an apparently insignificant find tells a story, poses a riddle, and thereby stimulates my mind.

Among my beach treasures are shells, undamaged or broken into sculptural fragments; pieces of sand-scoured driftwood silky to the touch; feathers of sea birds, often tattered, symbolizing by their battered condition the power of storm-tossed waves; carapaces of horseshoe crabs, those living fossils, those ultra-conservative anthropods that haven't changed for 175 million years, testifying to the stability of successful adaptations; pieces of coral that look like aggregates of tiny flowers; pebbles of many sizes and colors, rounded and polished by rolling waves; bones of fish or water fowl, three-dimensional stress diagrams that reveal with uncompromising clarity to the initiated eye the forces they are designed to withstand; starfish and sand dollars with their radial symmetrical forms—they testify that nature has a seemingly infinite number of ways to adapt life's representatives to any kind of environment.

A section of the beach near Westport, Connecticut. Strewn with sea wrack piled up in rows, this shore to me is a gold mine where I find such treasures as: shells entire or broken into bits of "sculpture," starfish, feathers of sea birds, fish bones, driftwood, surf-polished pebbles, shells of lobsters and crabs.... a never ending, stimulating collection of small objects of nature, grist for my close-up camera.

These natural beach sculptures can be approached from two viewpoints, each requiring a different language for understanding: the viewpoint of the scientist to whom they speak of the forces that shaped them, of the stresses and strains which they were designed to withstand, and of the purpose that gave them their functional, invariably effective form. Or they can be approached from the viewpoint of anyone receptive to beauty regardless of purpose or meaning—any artistically inclined person to whom it doesn't matter what the respective object represents or is called as long as it possesses that rare and precious quality which can give pleasure to the senses and satisfaction to the mind: beauty.

One of my favorite beach treasures is the sun-bleached skull of a gull, which I keep in front of me on my desk. While I admire its sculptural beauty, its history piques my imagination. I can picture its former owner gliding above gray waves, eyes filling the now empty sockets scanning the sea, powerful wings with even strokes parting the air, carrying the bird in soaring, effortless flight. I close my eyes and imagine being a gull myself. I feel weightless, floating on airfoil wings, a mood of peace and happiness pervades my soul.

Flanked by two small shells, which give it scale, a stone rounded and polished by the ceaseless grinding of rolling waves, looms monumentally against the sky.

Seen from ground level, a broken conch shell rises dramatically toward the clouds.

Stuck in the sand and seen from below, the three-inch jawbone of a fish reveals its sculptured elegance.

A bone from an
angler fish. With the
clarity of a three-
dimensional stress
analysis, its structure
depicts the strains and
stresses it is designed
to withstand.

A broken conch shell seems to greet an approaching storm with open arms—a symbol reminding me of certain modern abstract sculptures.

A Venus comb murex shell.

The limy skeleton of a coral.

103

A lump of coral.
Marvel at the intricate
design of the tubes in
which the polyps live.

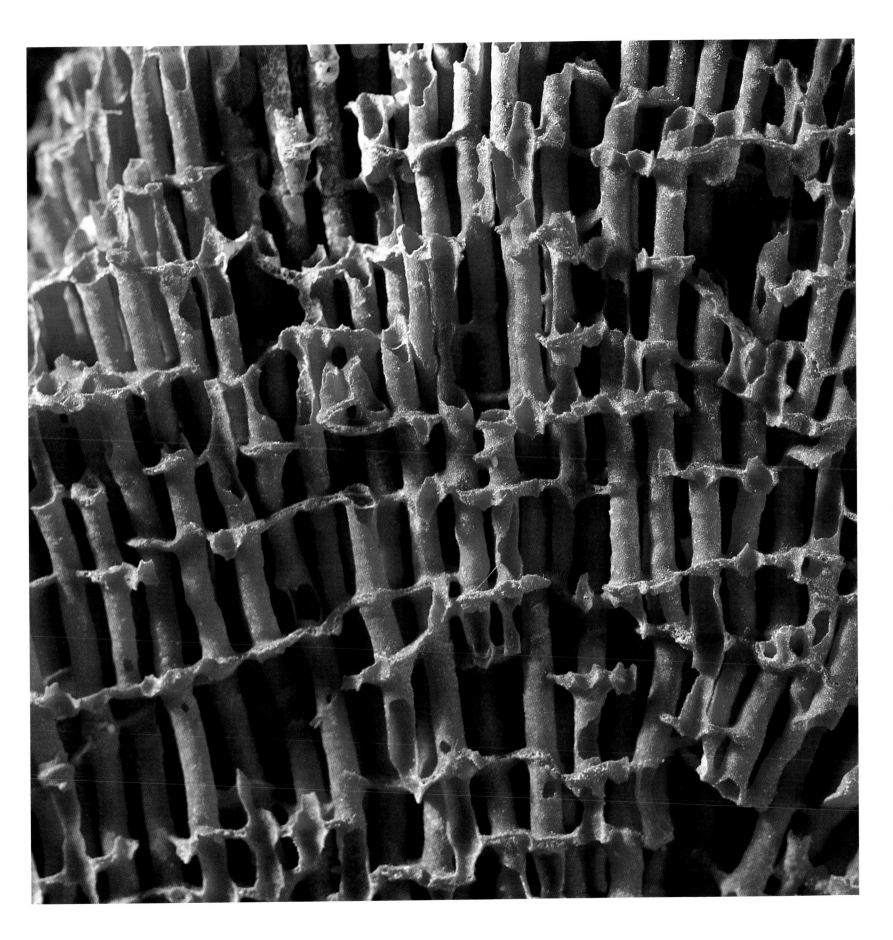

Pieces of granite from the end moraine of an ice-age
glacier deposited at the beach near Montauk Point,
Long Island, New York. Each stone is ground to almost
geometrical perfection by the ceaseless rolling action of
the surf.

Calcareous skeletons of tube worms make a lacy design
on a stone thrown upon the beach by a storm.

A gull skull on a chunk of driftwood, a monument in honor of the sea.

109

A clam shell, eroded and broken, reveals its internal
structure.

The skull and weather-beaten feathers of a gull against the background of a stormy sky combine to symbolize the hardship of life on the sea.

Down feathers of
Canadian geese gently
drift to earth.

Down feathers lit by
the last rays of the
setting sun.

A broken conch on a pebble polished by the sea, a monument in miniature.

A piece of driftwood
pointing out to sea.

An animal vertebra in the sand.

Symbolism
and
Imagination

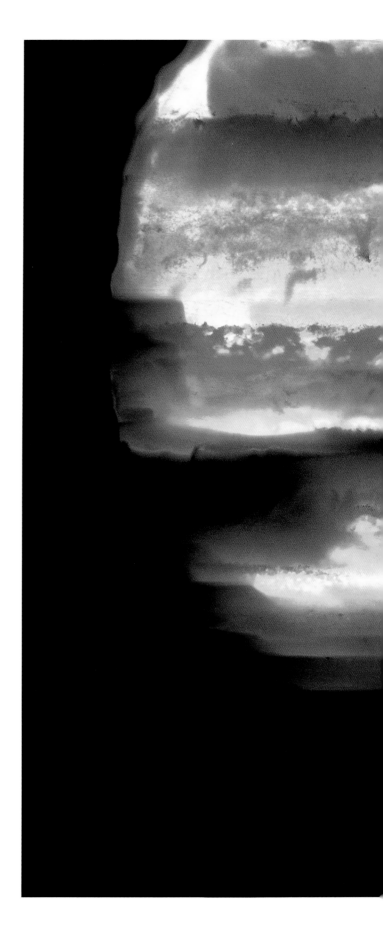

A thin slice of transluminated agate—or clouds at
sunset on another planet?

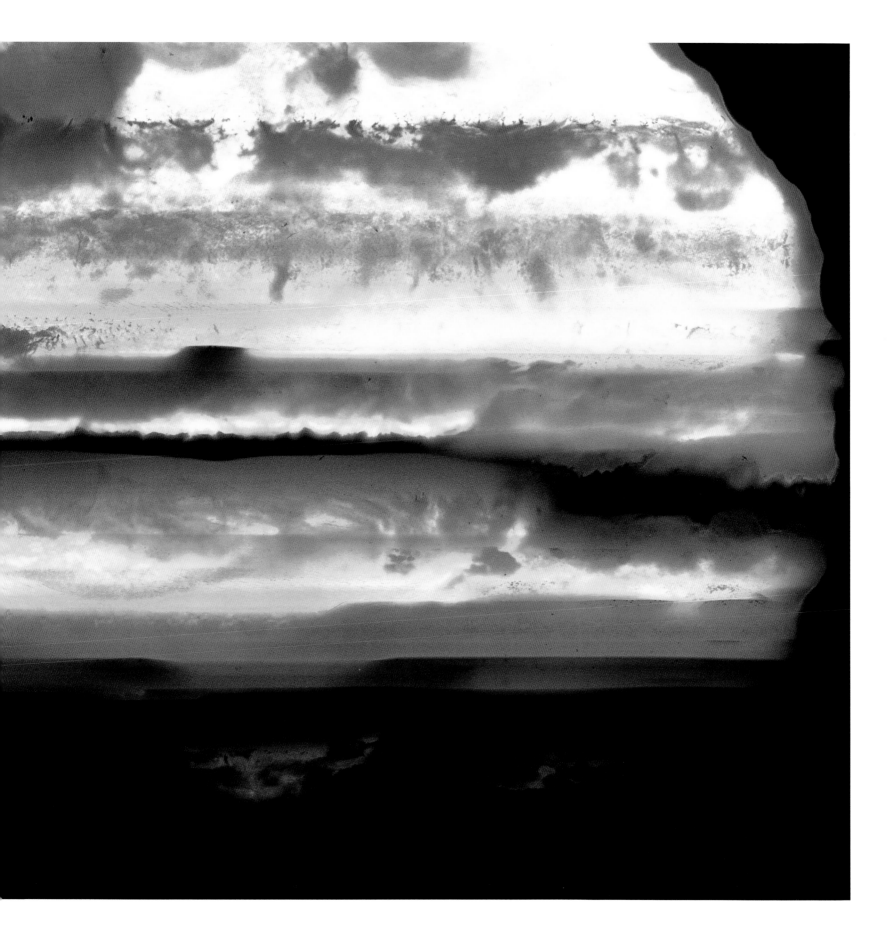

A symbol is an object which stands for an intangible—a thought, a concept, a sound, a belief, a figment of the imagination. Imagination is the ability to form mental images.

In my search for subject matter suitable to illustrate specific aspects of reality, I sometimes come up with objects that affect me in two ways: they literally suit my purpose, but they also remind me of something totally unrelated to the matter at hand. And thus they become symbols. The images in this chapter possess these dual qualities. I will try to convey, by means of the picture language of photography, some of the thoughts that entered my mind when confronted with certain objects of nature.

The subjects depicted in this chapter vary widely but all have one quality in common: they symbolize to me concepts normally buried below the level of everyday thought. Some, like animal skulls, the backbone of a bird, or a stone crossed by veins of quartz, reminded me of spirits of the forest, demonic faces, totem poles, or mystic rune-like designs. Others, like pieces of driftwood, called forth erotic connotations. In certain minerals, I saw otherworldly landscapes. They brought to mind scenery I had encountered in dreams. They are caricatures of earthly landscapes and skies—fantastic, unreal, and weird, like images brought back from a journey to outerspace.

Whenever necessary to express my experiences, I carried photographic symbolism one step beyond the conventional to indicate such intangible qualities as monumentality, the feeling of freedom associated with sea and sky, worship and awe toward spirits and gods, thoughts triggered by similarities between objects and mental concepts, and so on, by deliberately exaggerating or suppressing a subject's scale, assuming an unusual angle, working with unorthodox subject positions, or other creative means of composition. Methods like these permit me to exploit photography to the fullest, raising it from a simple medium of reproduction to a sophisticated means of communication capable of expressing feelings and thoughts.

The porcupine-gnawed skull of a woodchuck half-hidden in the moss— or a totem personifying the spirit of the forest worshipped by a primitive tribe?

A catfish skull—or a
representation of the
demonic forces in
nature?

The symbol of the
cross eternally fixed in
granite and quartz.

123

The backbone of a little bird and a woodchuck skull, functional sculptures of nature. Contemplate them long enough, and there is no end to the variety of images and thoughts they evoke.

Acorns—symbols of fertility, of women's breasts, of the
continuity of life.

Driftwood on a lonely beach—or phallic symbols created by nature herself?

128

Brecciated limestone—or a view of a valley seen in a
dream?

Right: Mica with inclusions of hematite and pyrolusite—or a
modern abstract painter's concept of a group of trees?

A thin slice of chalcedony seen in transmitted light—or
the image of an erupting volcano not of this world?

132

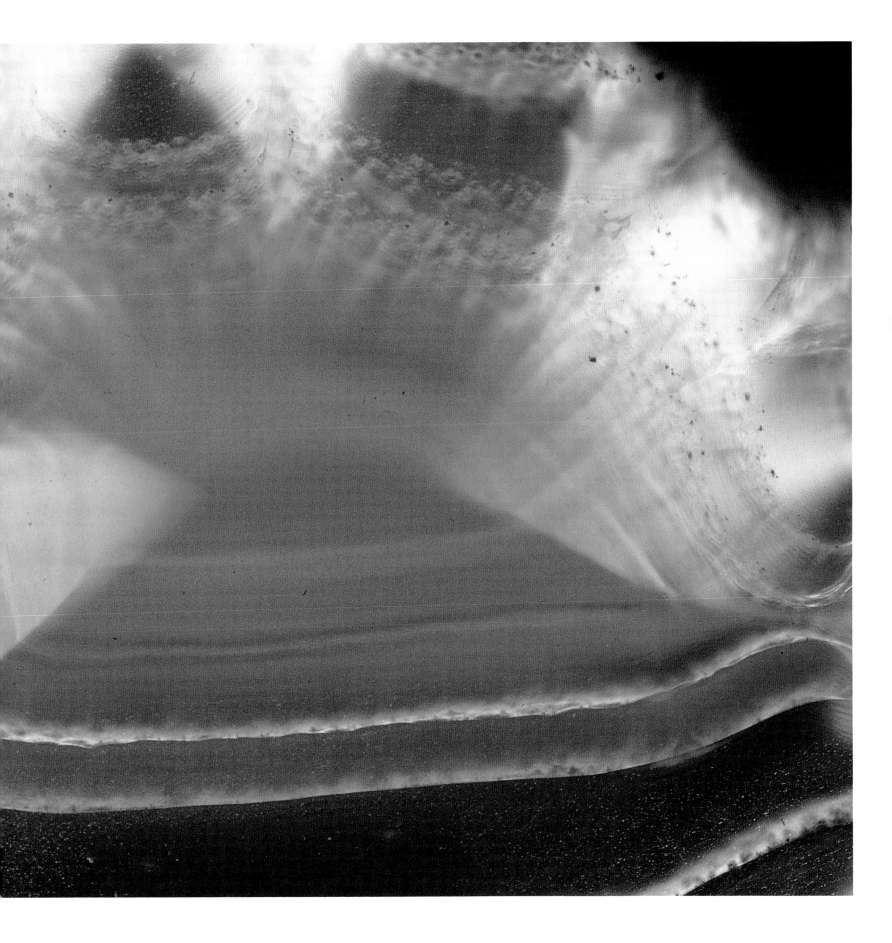

Transluminated agate slice—or a scene from the
Inferno?

Traces of gold in lapis lazuli from a stone in a woman's ring—or a galaxy beyond Andromeda?

135

A flat piece of sandstone—or rolling foothill country, a summer sky, a gentle breeze?

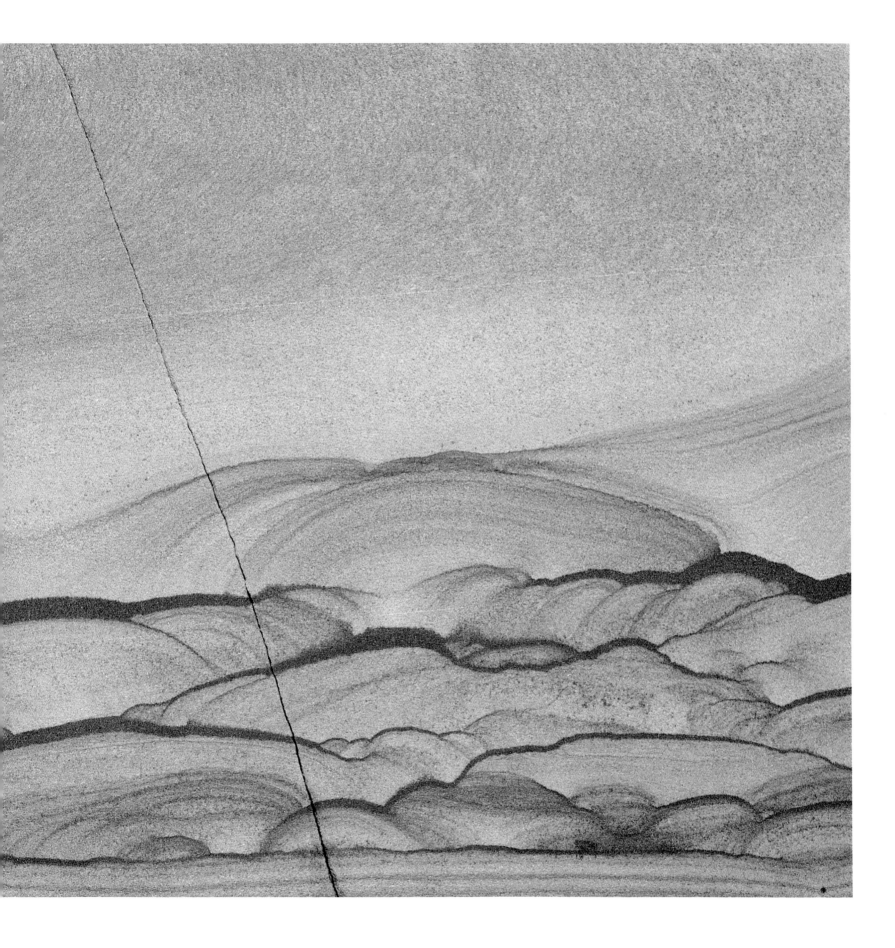

Thin slices of polished
agate—or scenes
from an unknown
planet?

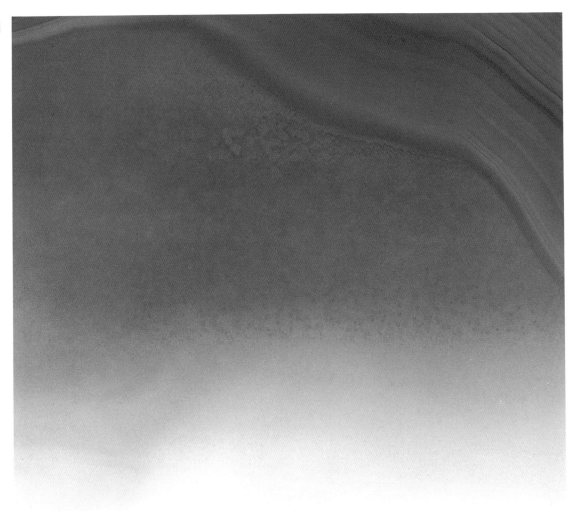

Epilogue

A piece of polished chalcedony—or a view from another world?

I am compelled to teach, to share with other people certain thoughts and feelings which I found both interesting and important, and the means most effective to accomplish my ends is photography. Photography allows me to communicate with anyone regardless of differences of alphabets, letters, or speech. Furthermore, the camera, although in certain respects inferior to the human eye, is superior in others: it can produce clear images of objects that are too far away or too small to be perceived by the unaided eye; it can arrest the fastest motion for subsequent study; and it can freeze time and allow me to analyze at leisure past events.

Creating picture books gives my life a purpose and a goal. What I hope to accomplish through them is to make people more aware of conditions which, for better or for worse, affect everybody's life. Because it makes me sick to read and hear almost daily about the destruction that human beings, out of ignorance or driven by need or greed, inflict on our environment. I want to show these people the beauty of the things they destroy, hoping to make them realize that other values exist besides the acquisition of wealth; that in the pursuit of monetary goals they destroy intangible values of health and happiness without which life is not worth living. I want to make these people care, because the things for which we care become precious, they are appreciated, respected, and preserved.

To cope with the frustrations of trying to reach these people, I persuaded myself that my books, in effect, are similar to flowers; both are ephemeral, both fulfill their destination without the slightest guarantee for success, both must rely on luck in regard to deposition and reception of their messages or seeds. And having done their work, they wilt and die, or go out of print and are remaindered, to be replaced by the next generation of flowers or books. In my case, the only certain reward is the memory of countless hours filled with joyful creative activity and the satisfaction of having done my best.

Summer, 1988
Andreas Feininger
New Milford, Connecticut